Design, Steph

BEATING THE BOUNDS

A policeman's account
of an ancient
Stockport ceremony
in 1854

By Joshua Brown
(1805 - 1904)

Stockport Heritage Publications in association
with Dr. Harcourt Brown of Winnipeg
1989

By 1810 mills and workshops were spreading below St. Mary's church. A windmill is just visible on the far right.

Introduction
by Harcourt Brown with R.B. Fleming

JOSHUA BROWN was born on 7th April 1805 at Fallowfield, which was at that time a village four miles from Manchester. He was a grandson of an East Anglian silversmith. Joshua's father, William Brown, was born in Norfolk and later fought as a British soldier in the American Revolution. Joshua himself seems to have been a blacksmith and teacher before joining the police forces of Manchester and Stockport, where from 1853 to 1855, he served as Superintendent of Police. In his spare time, he enjoyed writing, and left behind several narratives and "The System of the Universe or a Treatise on the Laws of Matter and Motion," published in 1854.

The development of industry was making Stockport, at least in Joshua's opinion, a less attractive place to live. In 1855, with his wife, Sarah Price, and nine children, he sailed to North America, which he had already visited, having spent several months in New York in 1841. In Toronto, Canada, he applied for the job of superintendent of the Toronto Police Force, but was offered instead the position of deputy superintendent, which he refused. He bought a piece of land in Norfolk County, near the village of Lynedoch in southwestern Ontario a few kilometres north of Lake Erie. Within a few years, Joshua and his family had developed a successful farm, which they called "Cranbrook Lodge".

In 1876, to commemorate the twentieth anniversary of the family's settling at Cranbrook Lodge, Joshua Jr. wrote a poem in which he recalled that "Twenty years and more have fled; Since this sod echoed first our tread." The children later lived in both Canada and the United States, and engaged in law, medicine, teaching, writing, and farming. My grandfather, John Price Brown, the most eminent of the family, won two gold medals when he graduated from the University of Toronto, and later practised as a nose and throat specialist in Toronto. He too was a writer. Five of his novels were published, their subjects ranging from the Rebellion of 1837 in Upper Canada to a novel about a pioneer Ontario doctor.

Joshua died in December 1904 at Cranbrook Lodge a few months short of his hundredth birthday. He never forgot the land of his birth. In February 1893, on the sixtieth anniversary of her parent's marriage, their daughter Ellen wrote a poem called "Jubilee" which evoked their lingering fondness for England. The third verse reads :

> Though in the West as time went round
> A wider heritage was found
> Yet fondly, lingering memory
> Clings to the country of their birth
> That grand old isle across the sea
> The dearest land on earth.

In 1854, the year before he left Stockport for Canada, Joshua Brown had helped to revive a tradition that had apparently lapsed for several years. Walking or "beating" the boundary of the township of Stockport had been a triennial ritual to verify the outer limits of the township, to settle any grievances arising over the demarcation lines and to enjoy an outing with friends and fellow officials of the town. As inspector of police, Joshua's role was to represent the law and to ensure its enforcement in case of disputes. Given the irregular streets and the uneven, often precipitous terrain of the town and its surrounding borough, the job of beating the boundary must have proved exhausting to all but the very fit.

With his keen eye for detail and his obvious enjoyment of recalling the event, Joshua recorded the day for posterity. The narrative has every sign of being written shortly after the event. He entitled it "Walking the Boundary of the township of Stockport, September 25th 1854." He refers to himself as "Mr. Brown, the superintendent of the borough police." Where necessary, we have added appropriate punctuation, but otherwise we have left the narrative almost exactly as Joshua Brown wrote it. In some cases, family and place names are unclear, and occasionally the editors have suggested alternative spellings. Residents of Stockport today may recognize ancestors and connections, and may wish to correct any mis-spelt names. Comments and further information would be welcomed from readers, as would further information on Joshua Brown or Sarah Price. Please address Dr. Harcourt Brown, 336 Kingsway Ave., WINNIPEG, Manitoba R3M 0H5, CANADA. Joshua Brown's papers are available for study at the Provincial Archives of Ontario, Toronto. Eric Angel is responsible for the transcription of the original document. John Price Erichsen-Brown, a grandson of Joshua Brown, deserves thanks for having preserved many of Joshua's papers.

Winnipeg, Canada
14 January 1989

A rural view of Stockport in 1790.

Mills encroaching along the river towards Brinksway in 1819.
The castle mill, left, and St. Peter's domed tower, centre, are visible.

Walking the boundary of the township of Stockport Sept. 25th 1854

by Joshua Brown

WALKING the boundary it seems may be done once in three years according to act of Parliament, the expenses to be charged to the overseers of the township, but in Stockport the practice has fallen into disuse, and this is the first boundary walking we understand which has taken place in this township for nine years. It is a pity such good old practices should be allowed to fall away, for they serve to keep up a good understanding amongst those persons who have to do with boundaries as the overseers and the different officials of the borough, as well as being right merry meetings ending in a good dinner.

The assembly took place at half past nine o'clock at the Bulkeley Arms [probably the Warren Bulkeley], and the procession commenced from the westerly side of the middle of Lancashire Bridge at 10 o'clock, headed by

Form of Character granted to Officers and Constables when wishing to apply for other Situations, whilst still holding their appointments in the Police Force.

TOWN HALL, MANCHESTER.

CHARACTER OF

Joshua Brown
Inspr. B. Division

21st Septr 1853

This is to Certify, that _Joshua Brown_ Aged _40_ Years, Height _5_ Feet _9_ Inches, Eyes _grey_ Hair _light brown_ Complexion _fresh_ a Native of _Manchester_ in the County of _Lancaster_ Served in the Manchester Constabulary Force from the _eighth of August 1843_ (forty three) to the _date hereof_ during which time his Conduct _has been that of an active, intelligent, and trustworthy Officer — Inspector Brown has permission to apply for the situation of Superintendent of Police at Stockport._

All Characters which are granted to the Officers and Constables of the Manchester Police are filled up, without any erasure.

NOTE.—If the Applicant should not obtain the Situation herein named, it is requested that this Character may be returned to him, as he is required in such case to deliver it back to the Chief Constable, and not allowed to use it again on a future occasion.

Dates of Appointment to the several Ranks held in the Manchester Police.

Supernumerary ———
Ordinary Constable _8 Aug 1843_
Merit Class Constable _1 Jany 1845_
Sergeant ———
Sub-Inspector _11 Sept 1845_
Inspector _27 March 1851_

Edward Willis
Chief Constable of the Borough of Manchester.

NOTE.—Extract from the proceedings of the Watch Committee.—See over.

A character testimonial from the Chief Constable of Manchester stating that Joshua was an "active, intelligent and trustworthy officer" the Mayor. There were present Messrs. Earnshaw [?], Newton and S.W. Wilkinson, overseers; Mr. Hunt, Borough Surveyor, Mr Thorniley of Heaton Norris, whom we are told walked the boundary fifty years ago, being then a Grammar school scholar; Mr. Cunningham and Mr. Jepson, assistant overseers; Mr. Boyle [?], Mr. Dodson and several other collectors and officials. We also noticed Mr. Brown, the superintendent of the borough police. Dr. Pearson was also present and several other gentlemen with a number of the Grammar school and British school boys, in all about 30 persons.

The procession moved along Great Underbank and Chestergate, on the right side, Mr. Hunt having explained before leaving Lancashire Bridge, that the boundary of the township lay down the middle of the river. At several openings to the river, we went down to the brink as near as possible, one of them being that place where the Tin Brook discharges itself, after working its way through an arch running under Church Gate, Hopes Carr, the Millgate etc. Mr. Leigh's mill gave us access to another part of the river, where we travelled along a stone embankment for some distance. The mayor, however, who was on horseback, rode round to a place where the township ends, and to get at which from our position required that we should ascend a wall some seven feet high. Mr. Gosling attempted this, but not being fully fledged, his pinions would not carry him over, and there he hung like Mahomet's coffin betwixt heaven and earth, until hauled over like a sack of flour by main force. Mr. Newton, the overseer, not having such "an unco slight of cauk and Neel" (probably old dialect meaning "not having over indulged in cakes and ale") mounted the wall gallantly, and the rest of us quietly walked round.

The township does not run up to Brinksway bridge, but terminates at, or about, a jutting point of rock which may be seen from the bridge, and which was once known as Neale's Ford. There is a slight stream of water still discharging itself near the same place, and which must at one time have been a stream of considerable magnitude, judging from the remains of a partly built up arch in that locality and still covering its course. The name of the stream appears to be lost, as no one in the company seemed to know it. This stream passes under the foundations of several houses, runs across Chestergate, and through the grounds of Major Marsland where a grid in one or two places marks its course. From thence it runs into a field at the back and so on along the hedge side, until it comes out at Daw Bank and Shaw Heath, near the house of Mr. Coppock. Whether the same stream marks the boundary still I cannot tell, but the course we took was up Shaw Heath until we came to some premises leading to the catholic chapel about the middle of which is the boundary line. From thence we went straight across the street, and through a garden, and along a hedge until we came out at 62 Greek Street, which is the last house in Stockport on that side. We then went along the street by the end of Spedding's beer house, and so on to a boundary post near where the

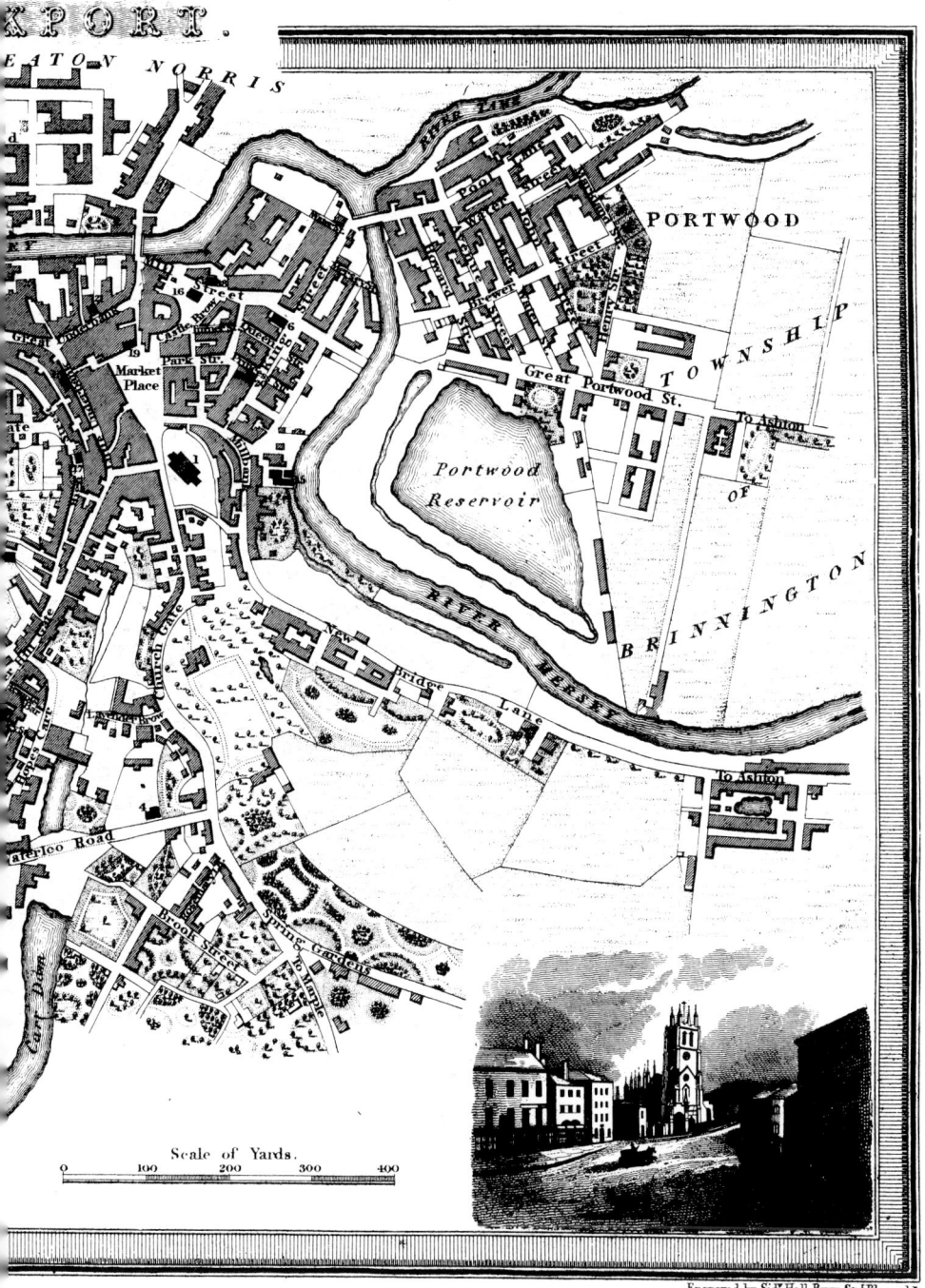

A panorama of Stockport from Heaton Norris in 1830 shows the spread of mills and smoky chimneys. Sited below the parish church, left, is the castellated muslin mill, visible above the trees.

Centre of the skyline is the bulk of Stockport Sunday School - largest in the country. Right is the recently built Wellington Road, passing two large mills, the lower, Wellington Mill, still stands today.

railway ceases to be tunnelled over. From thence we struck into the fields and took a zigzag course along the hedges to Adswood Lane; across the lane through a garden and again through fields until we reached Kenworthy Grave Lane the course being marked here and there by boundary posts standing in the hedge backs. This lane led us to the turnpike on Buxton Road at Mile End when we had the township of Bramal [Bramhall] on our right side and Stockport on the other, Stockport however claiming the whole of the road. This continued until we came to the tollbar, where we passed through a garden behind the bar and again struck into the fields. Now our journey lay along the hedge rows as before, and betwixt crushing through hedges, leaping ditches, and gathering blackberries, we found ourelves pretty well employed having to make many a sharp run to keep up with Mr. Hunt, who only now and then stopped to point out something to be borne in mind particularly. This route terminated in a lane, which again terminated in Offerton Lane at the commencement of Hempshaw Lane. Here some dispute took place about which was the true boundary line, Mr. Cunningham making a note to be referred to again at the next meeting. We now crossed Offerton Lane, and again crossed the fields by the hedge rows to a farm house near Mr. H. Marsland's park wall, and into a lane running along the wall, the lane being out of the township of Stockport, and with the park forming a portion of the township of Bredbury. We thus went on until the boundary line ran through the centre of a farm house, belonging to Mr. Marsland, I believe. From this house it took the centre of a shrubbery terminating at a steep woody hill side, termed Wood Side, and near Mr. Marsland's park gates. Wood Side leads down to the river Mersey or Goyte; there seems to be some dispute which, but that did not prevent us from tumbling down the steep declivity over the shoe tops in mud and clay, holding on by twigs and bushes in the best way we could, until we finally reached the river side. Here a man was stationed to swim the river, as the boundary lay right across, just above a wear (weir?) in the river, and opposite to which on the other bank is a boundary post. From this the line runs into the river and through the pier of the bridge at New Bridge Lane. According to another boundary post it again leaves the river on the same side, but Mr. Hunt thought that the line continued along the stream to a point opposite the hedge terminating a field running up to the road and through which we had walked after leaving New Bridge Lane. The boundary is round this field to some buildings bordering New Bridge Lane, when it again strikes off towards the river, and through the garden of a farm house where a boundary post is fixed, and where there are the remains of an ancient ford on the opposite bank. From this the line takes the centre of the river to Lancashire Bridge, the Easterly side of which we reached about 3 o'clock where our journey terminated.

    At half past four we sat down to an excellent dinner and wine at the Bulkeley Arms, and spent together a very pleasant evening, thus terminating what was altogether an exciting and agreeable day.

Woodbank Hall in 1850, the home of Mr. Marsland, near the "steep declivity".

Dr. John Price Brown, Harcourt Brown, Newton Brown and Joshua Brown - four generations in 1903.

photo in possession of Harcourt Brown

Manchester police on parade in the 1840's when Joshua was a Constable.

Off duty Constables taking a pipe.

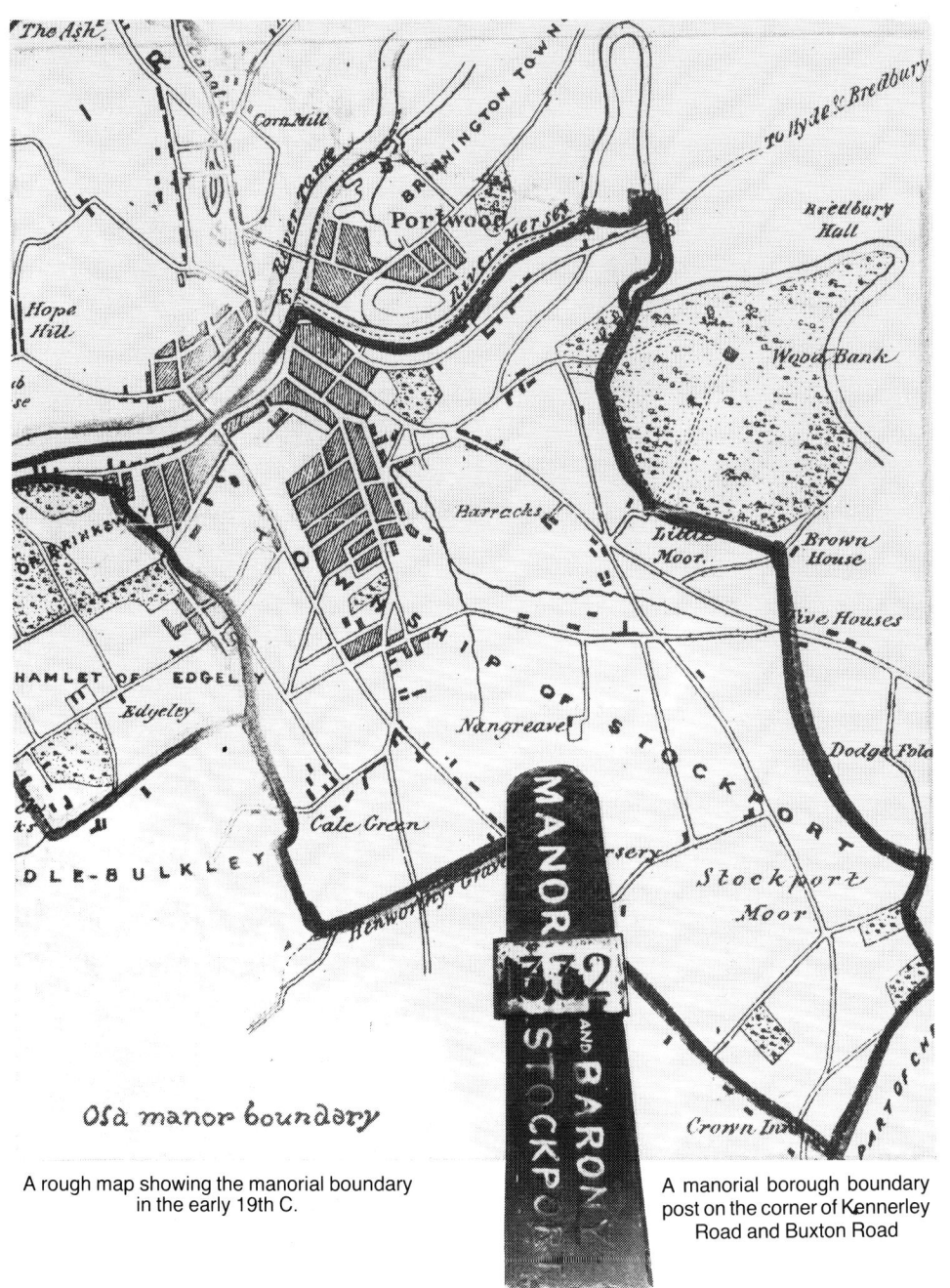

A rough map showing the manorial boundary in the early 19th C.

A manorial borough boundary post on the corner of Kennerley Road and Buxton Road

Note on the Editor

Harcourt Brown, Joshua's great grandson, received his education at the University of Toronto and Columbia University and subsequently taught briefly at Queen's University, Brooklyn College, the University of Rochester, and Washington University. From 1937 to 1969 he was Professor of French Language and Literature at Brown University, Providence, where he now holds the position of Professor Emeritus.

Dr. Brown was co-founder and associate editor of **Annals of Science (London)** (1935 - 1974) and a member of the board of editors of the **Journal of the History of Ideas (1944 - 1976)**. He is the author of **Scientific Organizations in Seventeenth-Century France** (1934, 1967) and **Science and the Human Comedy** (1976) and the editor of **The Army's Mister Brown: A Family Trilogy** (1982). He has been a member of numerous academic associations, including the History of Science Society, the Modern Language Association of America, the Modern Humanities Research Association, and the Académie des Sciences, Arts et Belles-Lettres de Caen. He has published articles in a wide variety of journals and reference works including the **University of Toronto Quarterly**, **Studies in the Renaissance**, **Studies in Voltaire and the 18th Century**, **Diogenes**, **Isis**, the **Journal of Higher Education**, the **Journal of the History of Ideas**, the **Revue d'Histoire de la Littérature française**, the **Bulletin de la Société d'Histoire du Protestantisme français**, **Daedalus**, the **Dictionary of Scientific Biography**, the **Rendiconti** of the Accademia Nazionale dei Lincei in Rome, and **Annals of Science**. He currently lives in Winnipeg and is active in the academic life of that city.

EXPLORE THE PAST & PRESENT !

Stockport Heritage Magazine

is available from Newsagents
and Bookshops

Subscriptions for 4 issues £5.50 (Overseas £7.50)

From : Stockport Heritage Publications
12, Devon Close, Stockport SK5 8DD